AF266636

Candy Motzek, BASc, PCC

Say YES TO YOUR BEST LIFE

31 DAYS TO CLARITY,
CONFIDENCE AND CONTENTMENT

ISBN: 978-1-9994814-2-1

Disclaimer: The information in this book is for entertainment purposes only and does not constitute health advice in any way. Readers should consult with their own medical professionals before embarking on any health or mindset training.

Published by Step Into Success Now Publishing
The author of this book can be reached as follows:

Candy Motzek
stepintosuccessnow.com

First edition February 2019

Contents

Introduction   **1**

Start Here   **5**

DAY 1 Practical Self Care   15

DAY 2 Daily Gratitude Practice   21

DAY 3 Morning Ritual   25

DAY 4 Create Your Own Personal Sanctuary   29

DAY 5 Meditation: Body Scan   33

DAY 6 Quiet Your Inner Critic   37

DAY 7 Meet Your Wise Self, the Inner Mentor   43

DAY 8 Know Your Values. Feel More Satisfied   51

DAY 9 Toxic People   55

DAY 10 Jumpstart Your Confidence   59

DAY 11 Eliminate Limiting Beliefs   63

DAY 12 Meditation: Mindful Breathing   69

DAY 13 Turn It Off   71

DAY 14 How Do You Spend Your Time?   73

DAY 15 It's A Play Day   79

DAY 16 A Reverse To Do List 83

DAY 17 What Makes Your Heart Sing? 87

DAY 18 Create a Digital Vision Board 95

DAY 19 Eliminate Hidden Time Wasters 101

DAY 20 Get Honest and Unstuck 105

DAY 21 One Hundred Things That Make You Proud 109

DAY 22 Shift Beyond Stuck 113

DAY 23 Clear The Clutter 117

DAY 24 Let Go Of The Past 119

DAY 25 Take A Mindful Walk Outside 123

DAY 26 Learn How To Apologize 125

DAY 27 Journal Your Way To Inner Peace 127

DAY 28 The Most Powerful Word. NO! 129

DAY 29 You Deserve A Play Day 133

DAY 30 Write A Compassionate Letter To Yourself 137

DAY 31 Take Yourself On A Date 141

Conclusion **145**

About the Author **146**

INTRODUCTION

Welcome to my community. I'm so glad you're here.

I'm Your Personal Life Coach, Candy Motzek, and I look forward to hearing about you and your journey. Just like you, I've had ups and downs. Times of great joy and huge disappointment, grief and frustration. Through it all, personal growth has been critical to my happiness and inner peace. This book includes some of my all-time favorite exercises gathered over the years during my own journey and I'm so happy to share them with you.

My wish is for you to connect more deeply to your inner message and life purpose. I hope this book supports you in creating a completely fulfilling life.

This book is organized with one bite sized entry per day. How you approach it is completely up to you. You can do one exercise every day, or fast forward by doing more than one exercise per day. Alternatively, you can take a more leisurely pace. Whatever is best for you. Each day's exercise takes between ten and thirty minutes. Some days I ask you repeat an exercise for a few days to get the most benefit. I've designed the book to be useful both now and in the future. You're always growing, and as you learn and experience more, you may want to come back and redo this 31-day series from time to time.

I highly recommend you set aside the same time each day to read and do the exercise for the day. Many days there are questions for you to answer to deepen your learning. I recommend keeping the exercises in one place, either a three-ring binder that you dedicate to this challenge or a blank notebook, your Soul Journal.

It can be tempting to *think* about what you would write and to *think* these exercises through. However, you will get the most benefit if you **do** each exercise and write your answers. There is power in seeing what you've written and a sense of accomplishment when you begin to see how your life improves.

I recommend that all my clients always keep a Soul Journal, it's a lined notebook that you use throughout the month. Keep it with you to capture your light bulb moments or inspired thoughts. Get one you really like, something attractive is always more engaging.

My personal favorites are Moleskine notebooks. They're a sturdy journal that come with a ribbon bookmark. The acid free paper is great to write on, and they have an elastic closure as well as an expandable interior pocket. It's the perfect size to slip in my purse and I can jot down ideas anytime I have an 'aha' moment. They come in all sizes and colours choose a colour that inspires you.

Say YES to Your Best Life; 31 Days to Clarity, Confidence and Contentment is more than a book to read, put down and forget, the power of this book lies in the benefit you will get from doing the daily exercises. Within these pages, there are resources: **https:// bit.ly/2RWpRfY**. When you download these resources, it will make the experience more valuable. I want you to "hear" me in your mind, throughout this book and in the resources since I write in my real and completely unvarnished way. This is *exactly* how I show up with my private one on one clients. You will get the experience of being coached by me just by reading and participating.

I'm excited to become part of your personal growth and I want to stay close, to motivate you to enjoy the process of rediscovering who you are and refreshing your life.

Let's get started!

Your Personal Coach

Candy Motzek
Step Into Success Now
Stepintosuccessnow.com

START HERE

You're here for a reason. You want to be happy, have clarity, confidence and contentment. In a nutshell, you want to start living the life you were born to live. Maybe you know exactly what's not working. Maybe it's a vague sense of "something isn't right" or perhaps you are just plain stuck in a rut and want to get moving!

Let's start with an assessment of your life today and identify what will make you happier.

Many people wait until January 1st to establish a goal or resolution. But everyday can be a new beginning and there's nothing stopping you from making TODAY the first day of your New Year.

We'll start Day 1 tomorrow, but today where are you exactly??? Let's look at 8 key areas of your life together.

Download the Free Resources that come with this book by going to **https://bit.ly/2RWpRfY.** You will get a copy of a printable PDF called "The Wheel Of Life" where you can easily take this assessment.

STEP 1: TO START, I'VE SELECTED THESE 8 LIFE ZONES:

√ Money.

√ Career / Business.

√ Personal Growth.

√ Love and Romance.

√ Friends and Family.

√ Physical Environment.

√ Health.

√ Fun and Recreation.

The table below gives you a brief description of the meaning of each zone.

LIFE ZONE	DESCRIPTION
CAREER/SCHOOL	WORK AND SCHOOL, INCLUDING YOUR CURRENT JOB AND CAREER PATH, VOLUNTEER ACTIVITIES
MONEY	INCOME, SAVINGS, DEBT LEVEL, INVESTMENTS, DISPOSABLE INCOME
FAMILY & FRIENDS	FAMILY, EXTENDED FAMILY, PARENTING, CHILDREN, YOUR SOCIAL CIRCLE
LOVE	THE LOVE AND ROMANCE IN YOUR LIFE
PERSONAL GROWTH	SELF AWARENESS, SPIRITUALITY, CHOOSING NEW BEHAVIOURS AND LEARNING NEW HABITS
FUN & RECREATION	RECREATION, HOBBIES, SPORTS AND CREATIVE PURSUITS
PHYSICAL ENVIRONMENT	WHERE YOU LIVE: CITY, COUNTRY, URBAN OR RURAL, NEIGHBOURHOOD, HOUSE OR APARTMENT
HEALTH	HEALTH, PHYSICAL FITNESS, DIET, WEIGHT, SLEEP AND ENERGY LEVEL

FOR EACH OF THE EIGHT LIFE ZONES, RESPOND TO THIS QUESTION.

HOW SATISFIED ARE YOU WITH THIS ZONE OF YOUR LIFE?

The rating scale is from 1 to 10 where 1 is horrible and 10 means it's more wonderful than you could have ever imagined. What's the first number that pops into your head? Move quickly, fill in the Wheel of Life. This part of the exercise will take less than three minutes.

Now connect the dots to create a shape within your Wheel of Life. This is a bird's eye view of your current life. Here's an example of a complete Wheel Of Life.

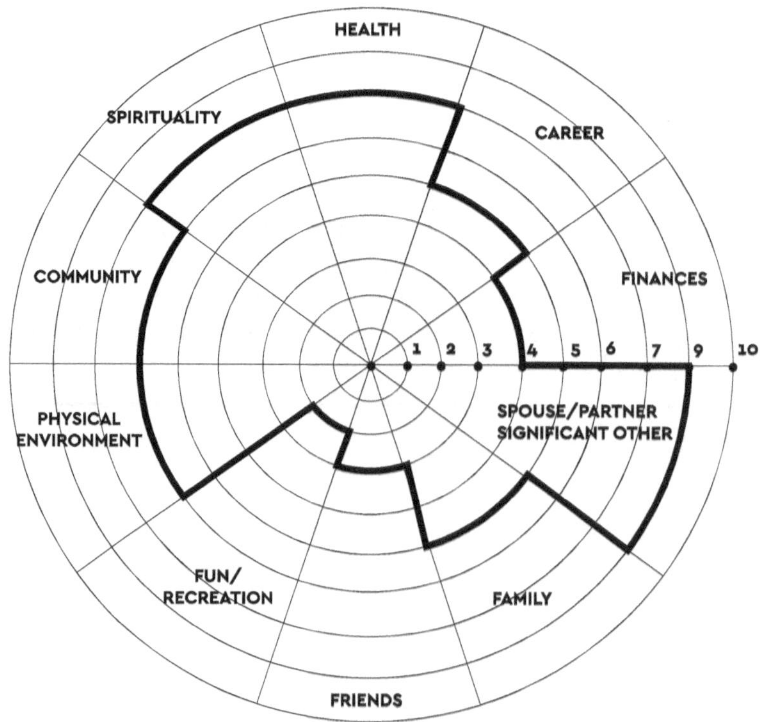

What's it like to drive your life on a wheel of this shape? Write your response in your Soul Journal. Is it bumpy, like driving on a flat tire, or does your wheel have to turn many revolutions for you to make any progress?

What do you notice about the shape of your life's wheel? Is it a surprise?

____

____

____

____

____

STEP 2: You are developing a snapshot of your satisfaction level, a bird's eye view of your life. Review your ratings and respond to these questions.

What do you notice about these scores? Is there a trend?

____

____

____

____

____

Are all the scores very low or very high? Or are there one or two scores that are very high, but because of an imbalance in your life the other areas have been ignored?

____

____

____

____

____

____

Seeing it on paper provides an entirely new perspective. What have you learned from this exercise so far?

____

____

____

____

____

____

STEP 3: if you need more room, write in your Soul Journal.

LIFE ZONE	WHAT DO I LIKE?	WHAT DO I NOT LIKE?
CAREER/SCHOOL	1 _______________ 2 _______________	1 _______________ 2 _______________
MONEY	1 _______________ 2 _______________	1 _______________ 2 _______________
FAMILY & FRIENDS	1 _______________ 2 _______________	1 _______________ 2 _______________
LOVE	1 _______________ 2 _______________	1 _______________ 2 _______________
PERSONAL GROWTH	1 _______________ 2 _______________	1 _______________ 2 _______________
FUN & RECREATION	1 _______________ 2 _______________	1 _______________ 2 _______________
PHYSICAL ENVIRONMENT	1 _______________ 2 _______________	1 _______________ 2 _______________
HEALTH	1 _______________ 2 _______________	1 _______________ 2 _______________

STEP 4: Choose three life zones you want to improve. Write down one action step for each that will increase your level of satisfaction. Make it something tangible. If I were to look over your shoulder would I know when you achieved it?

LIFE ZONE	ACTION I WILL TAKE
EXAMPLE: PHYSICAL ENVIRONMENT	I WILL BEGIN LOOKING FOR A NEW APARTMENT TO RENT CLOSE TO A PARK IN A BETTER NEIGHBORHOOD
EXAMPLE: HEALTH	I WILL DRINK HOT WATER WITH LEMON FIRST THING IN THE MORNING TO BOOST MY HEALTH.

STEP 5: Congratulations! You've just set three SMART goals. They are specific, measurable, action oriented, have a result and a time limit. Another more evolved way to describe the acronym SMART is simple, meaningful, awe inspiring or authentic, refreshing and thrilling.

ACCOUNTABILITY IS ONE OF THE BEST WAYS TO STICK WITH YOUR GOAL UNTIL YOU SUCCEED. CHOOSE AN ACCOUNTABILITY PARTNER TO KEEP YOU ON TRACK.

DAY 1
Practical Self Care

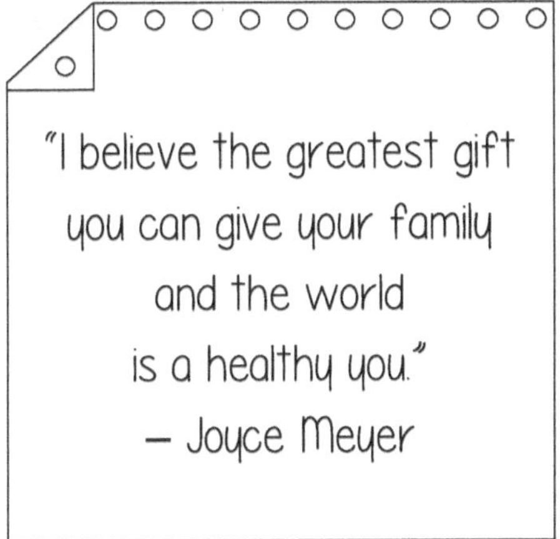

The first five days correspond to five foundational pieces to refresh your life. Today's topic is self care. Self care is one of the easiest things to be put on the back burner. Regular self care is key to being resilient, healthy and happy.

Create a list of ways to nurture and care for yourself.

Try one item from your list every day and see which you prefer. 31 days and 31 different ways to care for yourself will help you establish the habit that your well being is top priority.

Record your daily self care practice in your Soul Journal. Was it a boring, did you enjoy it, do you want to do it again?

This way you will create your own personalized self care tool kit to fall back on when you need a little boost of brightness and self love.

NEED SOME INSPIRATION? HERE ARE 99 SMALL AND PRACTICAL IDEAS FOR YOU TO TRY.

1. Spend time with your pet
2. Explore your town like a tourist
3. Go for afternoon tea
4. Have a bubble bath and place lit candles in the bathroom
5. Buy yourself a bouquet of flowers
6. Read a book
7. Buy and read a beautiful magazine
8. Go outside for a walk
9. Spend time in nature
10. Write in your Soul Journal
11. Take a nap
12. Make a doctor's appointment you've been putting off
13. Spend time colouring in a colouring book
14. Call a friend
15. Get and give a hug
16. Paint your nails
17. Deep condition your hair
18. Put on your prettiest lipstick
19. Enjoy your favorite dessert
20. Have a cup of tea and put your feet up for 10 minutes
21. Watch an episode of your favorite TV show
22. Meditate
23. Apply a face mask
24. Put some of your favorite essential oils in a diffuser

25. Light a candle and pray

26. Change into something comfy and pretty

27. Take time to enjoy a craft

28. Knit with beautiful natural yarn

29. Create your sacred space

30. Write in your Morning Pages

31. Smile at yourself in the mirror and say a positive affirmation

32. Give yourself a rolling pin foot massage by putting the rolling pin on the floor and rolling your foot overtop

33. Get a pedicure. Choose a colour that's fun

34. Take three deep cleansing breaths

35. Create art

36. Play a game

37. Drink a cup of warm water with organic lemon and honey

38. Stretch for five minutes

39. Do yoga

40. Take time to eat lunch away from your desk

41. Have a coffee date

42. Use your favorite stress reduction app (Some of my favorites are: Pottery, Pocket Pond 2 and My Reef)

43. Take your vitamins

44. Drink a green smoothie

45. Watch the sunrise or sunset

46. Listen to nature sounds on the app e.g. Naturespace

47. Watch a motivational Ted Talk

48. Ask for help

49. Write a thank you note

50. Write a love note to yourself

51. Cook a new recipe you've been wanting to try
52. Eat more fruits and veggies
53. Notice what you're feeling, just notice, don't deny or distract
54. Have a movie night out
55. Exercise
56. Write down one short term goal
57. Change the background on your computer or your phone to an inspirational quote
58. Donate clothes you don't wear any more
59. Do a random act of kindness
60. Talk to your coach
61. Talk to your therapist
62. Get your annual physical
63. Hang a bird feeder where you can see it and enjoy the birds
64. Say no to something you don't want to do
65. Read an inspirational poem
66. Go on a retreat
67. Plan a mini staycation
68. Organize your desk
69. Spend some time close to water. Hang out by a lake, the ocean or a river
70. Start a new hobby
71. Plant an herb garden in your window
72. Cuddle
73. Download a funny audio book
74. Eat a meal off your best dishes
75. Drink your tea from a fine china cup
76. Walk outside barefoot in the grass

77. Put a plant in your work area

78. Cook a wonderful ample meal so you can enjoy easy left overs tomorrow

79. Give yourself a break: delete something from your to-do list

80. Find or create a sacred space

81. Smile at people when you're out and about

82. Listen to an uplifting podcast

83. Curl up with a hot water bottle on a cool evening

84. Wear something in a colour that you love

85. Visit an art gallery

86. Learn something new that has absolutely nothing to do with work

87. Go for a bike ride

88. Get a fish tank

89. Take time to look at the photos from your favorite holiday

90. Go to your local museum

91. Throw a ball for your dog

92. Go to bed an hour earlier

93. Get your hair done

94. Bake something tasty

95. Watch a good movie at home

96. Get a massage

97. Join a book club

98. Create a new playlist and dance to it

99. Go to the beach

Jot down the ones that appeal to you most in your Soul Journal and then schedule them in your calendar.

WHICH WILL YOU TRY TODAY? PLAN TO DO ONE SELF CARE ACTIVITY EACH DAY FOR THE NEXT 31 DAYS.

DAY 2
Daily Gratitude Practice

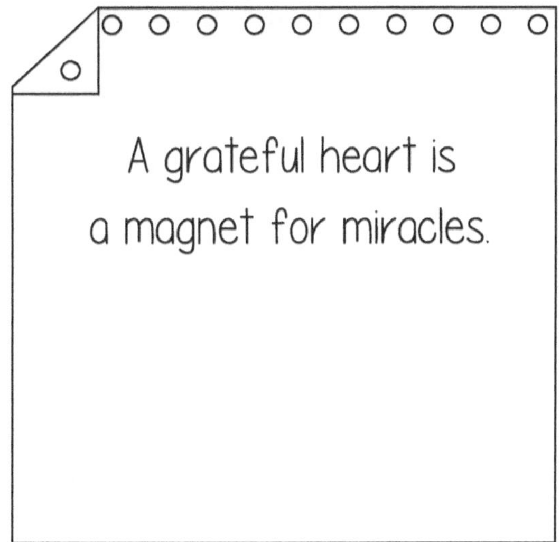

The biggest step you can take to increase your happiness is to include a daily gratitude practice. This is the reason I've selected this to be the second foundational piece of this program. At one of the lowest points in my life, I embraced gratitude as a defense mechanism because I was desperate. I was so tired of feeling sad and angry all the time. I started looking for things in my life to be happy about, because I was tired of feeling anxious and depressed.

Did you know research shows gratitude can even help you bounce back from trauma? On the outside your life can be exactly the same, but when you notice and capture the things you are grateful for it has a markedly positive effect on how you feel.

SIX SIMPLE STEPS TO MAXIMIZE A GRATITUDE PRACTICE:

Make A Commitment To Yourself

This is a practice that gains momentum with time. You can always find reasons to postpone doing it. Waiting for your resistance to pass or for it to be more convenient means it will never happen.

Gratitude is a cumulative practice. I suggest you practice for the next 30 days and you will notice a difference.

Start And Trust It Will Work Out

Sit down with pen and Soul Journal and write,

"I am grateful for" or "These things make me happy" or "I am thankful for" at the top of your page. Sometimes it will take a minute or two until you can think of something to write. Pause, reflect, and trust. The words will come, then write them down.

Write It Down, Everyday

There is power in putting pen to paper. Thinking about it or saying it isn't as effective as doing it. I get the most enjoyment from writing in my Soul Journal. Others are satisfied documenting it in their phone or on the computer. Experiment with what feels best for you.

2

Feel It

Some days you will write without feeling a shred of gratitude. That's ok. Just do it anyway. Whenever possible, as you write, summon up the feeling of gratitude in your heart, let it percolate through every cell in your body.

Choose A Time And Stick To It

Do you want to start your day or end your day with gratitude? I prefer to write my gratitude list first thing in the morning, while I sip my coffee. You'll know what's the right time for you. Be consistent, it helps to embed your new habit.

Allow Yourself To Be Human

Yes, you will make mistakes. When you miss a day or three (because it will happen) make a choice to begin again. The voice of your inner critic may say you've messed up and tell you not to bother because it's just a waste of time. Instead, tune into the still wise voice within you and pick up your pen and start anew.

STICK WITH IT,
THE BENEFITS ARE
WORTH IT. GRATITUDE
MAKES YOU HAPPIER,
HEALTHIER, IMPROVES
YOUR RELATIONSHIPS
AND BOOSTS YOUR
CONTENTMENT AND
SELF ESTEEM.

DAY 3
Morning Ritual

"I get up every morning and it's going to be a great day. You never know when it's going to be over so I refuse to have a bad day." —P. Henderson.

I love this quote, and it's true, how you start your day makes a huge difference to how you feel and how much you accomplish. The morning ritual is the third foundational piece for living a life of clarity, confidence and contentment.

Here's how my days used to begin. Does this sound familiar to you? I began my day when when my alarm went off, I would hit the snooze button three or more times. Before I dragged myself out of bed, I would lay there and complain about how much I didn't want to get up and how much I didn't like my job. Then, because I was late, I would jump in the shower, throw on some clean clothes, mascara and a bit of lipstick. Slurp a cup of coffee while I ran out the door for my morning commute. Does your morning sound something like this too?

How your day begin sets the tone for the entire day. During that time of my life I was always late, and I was never fully prepared. I sure wasn't showing up as "my best self". Plus, because I was rushing, my anxiety and stress levels were off the charts.

A few years ago, I created a fresh and healthier morning routine. With time I noticed that not only was I feeling better mentally and physically, I was also able to focus on my goals and get more done throughout the day.

Here's what a healthy morning routine looks like and some tips so you can try it too:

» No snooze button – when the alarm goes off, get up. Don't allow yourself to lay in bed.
» The 10-10-10 rule.
    » 10 minutes in either a mindful silence or gratitude practice.
    » 10 minutes reading something inspiring and...
    » 10 minutes moving, either go for a walk, stretch, do yoga. Turn on the music and dance in your pyjamas. Something to get my body moving for the day.
» Drink a cup of warm water and lemon before your first cup of coffee.
» Eat a healthy balanced breakfast. Some fruit, greens, egg whites, slice of whole wheat toast or oatmeal.

» Shower and dress in something that makes you feel good.

» Smile.

Adjust the 10-10-10 rule as you see fit. If you've got no time, make it the 5-5-5 rule. Are you seeing the benefits of this happy (for you) morning routine and want to amp it up? Make it the 20-20-20 rule.

Develop your own morning routine to stay positive, energized and focused. I found that because I no longer hit the snooze button I didn't even need to set my alarm earlier. For me, putting in the effort to establish this healthy morning routine made a big difference on my mood and my productivity. Give it a try and see how it changes your day!

IF YOU HAVEN'T ALREADY, REMEMBER TO DOWNLOAD THE FREE RESOURCES THAT I'VE CREATED FOR YOU TO MAKE YOUR EXPERIENCE WITH THIS BOOK EVEN MORE VALUABLE. USE THIS LINK TO ACCESS THEM NOW: **HTTPS://BIT.LY/2RWPRFY**

DAY 4
Create Your Own Personal Sanctuary

"Within you there is a stillness and sanctuary to which you can retreat at any time."
–Herman Hesse

Today, is the fourth of five foundational pieces in this program. This space goes by many names, a personal sanctuary, bliss space, sacred space, prayer nook, or personal altar. We all need a place where we retreat from the world and connect with our source.

It's a place to get centered and refreshed. It's a place you can withdraw to when life gets tough and you need a break and a place to unwind. A place that's just for you. It doesn't have to be spacious, although if you have a room you can dedicate, lucky you!!!

These are a few must haves;

» Dedicated Space – a room, a she shed, a converted closet, the corner of your bedroom. You don't need a lot of space, but it's important to have it clear of clutter and dedicated to your personal sanctuary. It's not ok to have your sanctuary double as the place where your laundry basket sits!

» Something to sit on – it could be a comfy chair or a meditation cushion.

» A table, any size will do. it's somewhere to place your cup of tea and book.

» Something alive. A flower, a plant or a mini fish bowl.

» Light – close to a window is best.

» Something to keep you warm when it gets cool. For example, a shawl of throw in your favorite colour.

Here are some nice to haves;

» Lighting a candle is a powerful symbol.

» Invoke your sense of smell with aromatherapy.

» A bookshelf to store your favorite books and journals.

» Inspirational artwork.

» Crystals and stones.

» Fairy lights.

» Yoga mat.

» Chimes, or crystal bowl.

» Soft furnishings (pretty cushions, curtains, mats).

MOST OF ALL GIVE YOURSELF

THE PERMISSION TO HAVE

YOUR OWN SPACE.

I ENCOURAGE YOU TO CLAIM IT.

IT'S OK TO TELL YOUR FAMILY,

THIS LITTLE CORNER OF THE

WORLD IS JUST FOR YOU!

DAY 5
Meditation: Body Scan

> Don't try to be someone,
> be yourself.
> That is what meditation
> should teach you.

This is the fifth and final foundational piece of the program. I spent years knowing that meditation was "good" for me and resisting it. I had every excuse in the book. Do any of these sound familiar

» No time.

» Too distracted.

» No space.

» Too difficult.

» What a bother!

During a troubled time, I needed to manage my stress levels and I didn't want to feel bad anymore, so I tried it. And I stuck with it.

Meditation helped me heal and it keeps me on an even keel no matter what is going on in my life. Meditation is the fifth of five foundational pieces that you will use throughout this program.

Meditation has a wide range of benefits. Every year researchers are identifying even more advantages! Meditation is not a religious practice. Here's a quick list of what it can do for you:

» Improve your stress level.

» Better sleep.

» Improve your body's metabolism. Help you maintain a healthy weight.

» Improve your mood. Counteracts anxiety and depression.

» Increases your attention span.

» Slows aging.

» Improve your immunity to colds and flu.

Meditation doesn't have to be a complicated. You don't have to sit with your legs twisted in the lotus position for thirty minutes in complete silence. I know how tough it can be to meditate when someone walks in and says everything from "Honey, I can't find my car keys" to "Mom, I'm hungry".

To get you started on the meditation path listen to the three-minute easy meditation that is included in your Free Resources Library. To get access at **https://bit.ly/2RWpRfY**. You can use it anytime you need a break. I encourage you to try it today and for the next few days.

CAPTURE YOUR
INSIGHTS AND THE
IMPACT IN YOUR
SOUL JOURNAL.

DAY 6
Quiet Your Inner Critic

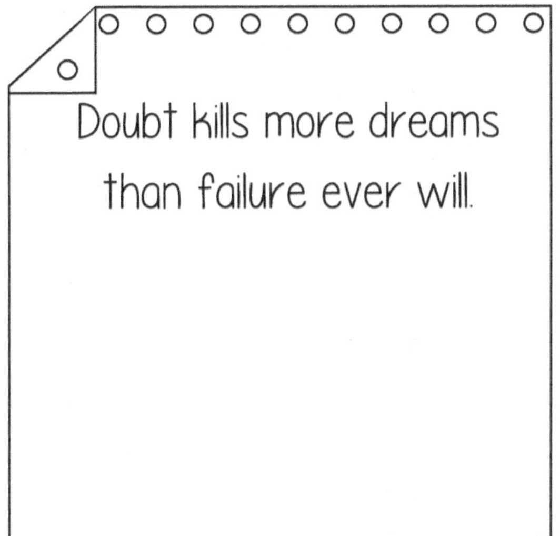

Your Inner Critic shows up when you want to strive for something new or make a change. Acknowledging and managing our Inner Critic is an important tool for awareness. Learning how to turn the volume down on your Inner Critic is one of the keys to contentment.

One way to look at the Inner Critic or the voice of your self doubt, it is a habitual way of thinking. Most Inner Critics were formed in childhood. The voice was integrated when adults were in charge and we never questioned their word. Those adults were probably trying to keep you safe from real danger, disappointment or to make sure you followed the rules. Sometimes your Inner Critic is a product of society's norms. As an adult, these limiting beliefs often stand in the way of your growth. It's safe to learn a new way. You can learn to question and make new decisions.

What does your Inner Critic sound like? It's the inner voice that says you're not good enough. The inner voice that makes you feel bad about yourself and keeps you tight and small instead of expansive and ready to strive for your goals. You may find your Inner Critic sounds like one of your relatives, maybe a school teacher or other authority figure from your childhood.

Often the Inner Critic uses the word "too".

For example, "you are too quiet or too boring or too loud", "you're too fat or too skinny", "you're too stupid to take that course". The Inner Critic wants to hold you back from trying something new or from playing bigger. It doesn't pull punches, it says mean things in your head that you would never say to anyone else.

Your goal learn how to identify the voice of your Inner Critic and how to turn down the volume on it.

COMPLETE THE QUESTIONS THAT FOLLOW.

What does your Inner Critic say to you?

____

____

____

____

____

____

When does your Inner Critic show up the most?

____

____

____

____

____

____

What does it repeat over and over like a broken record?

What about this is no longer true?

What's a new way to frame this limiting belief?

6

What do you want to do with this new information?

____

____

____

____

____

What's one action you can take to break free?

____

____

____

____

____

THE INNER CRITIC IS

DIMINISHED ONCE WE

RECOGNIZE IT AS AN

AUTOMATIC REACTION.

NOTICE WHEN IT SHOWS UP

AND REMIND YOURSELF TO

QUESTION WHY IT'S TRYING

TO KEEP YOU FROM PLAYING

BIGGER.

DAY 7
Meet Your Wise Self,
the Inner Mentor

"Deep at the center of our being is an infinite well of joy, an infinite well of love, an infinite well of wisdom."
— Louise Hay

Just as we have an outspoken Inner Critic, so too we have a wise and caring Inner Mentor. The Inner Mentor is a coaching tool I often use when faced with a choice. It's especially useful when you're part way to your goal and have stalled. Get to know this personal character it is empowering and will help you grow your confidence. Another name for this Inner Mentor is your intuition or your inner voice of wisdom. Everyone has one, but you need to learn to listen to the message.

How can you tell the difference between the voice of your Inner Critic and your Inner Mentor? The Inner Critic often talks in words and repeats the same message like a broken record. You hear the Inner Critic in your mind, and it makes you feel like you're not enough.

The voice of the Inner Mentor, or your intuition, can be quiet, simple and profound. The voice is more of a knowing that you feel in your heart or in your gut. You knew this voice when you were young. It's always speaking to you. The best way to learn to listen to the Inner Mentor's voice is with quiet persistence and practise.

Take a few moments to get centered by listening to your breathing.

ONCE YOU ARE CENTERED AND CALM, COMPLETE THESE QUESTIONS:

If you could step into anyone's shoes (living or dead) for half an hour, who would you choose for wise advice and counsel?

____

____

____

____

____

____

____

Take a moment and imagine that this person lives inside your heart. What advice would they give you?

____

____

____

____

____

Who else comes to mind that you would love to hear from?

____

____

____

____

____

What would they say?

____

____

____

____

____

Why do you look up to them?

Create a character that brings these role models together. What name would you call your Inner Mentor?

How does your Inner Mentor dress?

What does their voice sound like?

47

____

____

____

____

____

____

In your imagination, notice their strength, power and support. Notice how it feels to know they are always available and "on call" for you.

Again, close your eyes, take a few minutes to get centered. See your Inner Mentor clearly in your mind's eye. Imagine hearing their words and feeling their wisdom enter your heart. Know they are available for you anytime you need support. You can call on them for guidance and their wise loving energy will be there for you.

What special message do they have for you today?

48

____

____

____

____

____

____

Strengthen your relationship with your Inner Mentor. Daily connect with them by seeing them in your mind's eye. Frequently ask for their advice:

If you're confused, ask, what would my Inner Mentor have to say about this?

» What does your heart say?

» What does your gut know?

» Trust the message.

YOUR INNER MENTOR
WILL ALWAYS SPEAK
CLEARLY AND SIMPLY
TO YOU, ALL YOU
HAVE TO DO IS GET
CENTERED AND ASK.

DAY 8
Know Your Values.
Feel More Satisfied

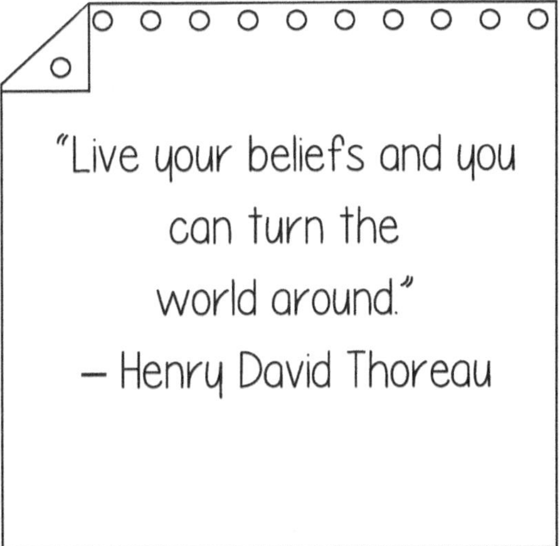

Living a life fully in alignment with your values never goes out of season. Your values are unique. People have told me that getting clear on their values is like building their life on an unshakable foundation.

What really matters to you? What is most important? What are the things that really push your buttons? These are all clues to your values.

HOW TO DO THIS EXERCISE:

STEP 1: Browse the values listed before and make a **note of the** ones that reflect who **you are** in your Soul Journal. I've **left some blanks** spaces as a reminder for you to consider any other values that are important to you.

ACCOMPLISHMENT	CREATIVITY	SELF EXPRESSION
ACHIEVEMENT	EXCELLENCE	HAPPINESS
CHALLENGE	CONNECTEDNESS	HARMONY
COLLABORATION	FREE SPIRIT	SPIRITUALITY
COMMUNITY	CONTRIBUTION	LIGHTNESS
DIRECTNESS	DOWN TO EARTH	NATURE
FAMILY	NURTURING	ADVENTURE
HUMOUR	SERVICE	FOCUS
INDEPENDENCE	SUCCESS	ACCURACY
INTEGRITY	BEAUTY	ORDERLINESS
JOY	LEADERSHIP	ZEST
PARTICIPATION	PERSONAL POWER	ROMANCE
PERFORMANCE	FREEDOM	RECOGNITION
PRODUCTIVITY	ACKNOWLEDGMENT	EMPOWERMENT
RISK TAKING	PEACE	TRADITION
ELEGANCE	GROWTH	VITALITY
AESTHETICS	TRUST	AUTHENTICITY

STEP 2: Now using your Soul Journal, narrow your list down to your top ten values and write them in the table next.

Ask yourself, "On a scale of 1 to 10, how much am I living true to this value now?" Add these scores to the table too.

If you scored less than seven for any of your top values, ask yourself. "What action can I take to bring more of this value into my life?"

	VALUE	RATING 1 - 10	IF YOU SCORE LESS THAN 7: WHAT ACTION CAN YOU TAKE IN THE NEXT MONTH TO BE MORE IN ALIGNMENT WITH THIS VALUE?
1			
2			
3			
4			
5			
6			
7			
8			
9			
10			

When you know your values, you make better decisions. When faced with a choice such as, "how do I decide whether to accept a job offer", "what should I major in at college" or "where should I go on my next vacation?" Use this simple approach. Ask; "which decision honors my values?" The response will help you to make the best decision and guide you to a more satisfied life.

AN EXAMPLE: One of my coaching clients was offered a huge promotion, but it involved moving to a new and very big urban area. She was flattered, then she took the time to look carefully at what this promotion would look like day to day. As she thought carefully about her life path, she realized it didn't honor her top values of family and nature. In addition, leadership and achievement were not among her top values. She declined the promotion and has since taken an alternate position close to her family in a smaller town.

DAY 9
Toxic People

"Toxic people defy logic. Some are blissfully unaware of the negative impact they have on those around them and others seem to derive satisfaction from creating chaos and pushing other people's buttons."
—Travis Bradberry

Our happiness and success are directly affected by the quality of our relationships. You know the saying "it's hard to soar like an eagle when you spend your day with turkeys." If you spend a lot of time with negative people it's going to be tough to get ahead, accomplish your dreams and be happy.

Choose to spend more time with people who support you and make you feel empowered. We've all got friends, co-workers and family who make us feel 'less than', guilty, depressed or drained. Awareness holds power. Sometimes it's as simple as taking a few minutes to figure out which people you want to be more connected to.

Here are some ideas of how to tell which of your relationships are toxic and which are sustaining. Once you are aware, then you can decide how you want to relate with them.

STEP 1: List the five people you spend the most time around in your Soul Journal.

STEP 2: Rate how you FEEL when you're around them? How do you FEEL when you leave them? Do you feel uptight, anxious, "less than", depressed, guilty or do you feel, nurtured and nurturing, full of laughter, calm, supported or playful? Your goal is to feel positivity as much as possible. To feel happy, light free, accepted, supported and loved.

How many of your close relationships don't feel that way? It can be a real eye-opener when you see this for the first time.

STEP 3: Identify your pattern. Once you see the theme you can decide what you would like to do. Who do you want to spend more time and invest more energy with?

STEP 4: Write one small simple action you will take.

For example, maybe you want to spend a little less time with your sister and a little more time with your friend. Maybe you notice your friend usually acts jealous when you share good news. Perhaps you could decide to share less with that friend because it always takes the wind out of your happy bubble. Maybe you would prefer lunch with one particular co-worker, because you always feel accepted and supported when you're with them.

NAME	HOW DO YOU FEEL WHEN YOU'RE AROUND THEM?	DO YOU WANT TO INCREASE OR DECREASE THE AMOUNT YOU CONNECT? (+ OR -)	WHAT SMALL ACTION CAN YOU TAKE TO MAKE THIS CHANGE?

Today's exercise is to help you choose who you spend time with and be judicious in who you share your life with. Living your best life means choosing to feel good.

I don't recommend that you reduce your relationships to a grading system, this <u>isn't a cut and dry exercise</u>. Nor do I recommend you cut ties with your negative family and friends, although you may occasionally decide that's best.

IT'S ABOUT
INCREASING YOUR
AWARENESS, SO YOU
CAN CHOOSE WHICH
PATH TO TAKE
THROUGHOUT
YOUR LIFE.

DAY 10
Jumpstart Your Confidence

"When you have confidence, you can have a lot of fun. And when you have fun you can do amazing things."
—Joe Namath

Today's tip is short.

Take a leap!

It's one of the fastest ways to boost your confidence and to feel fully alive. Even better, do something that is a little scary! Ok, I can feel you getting all tense as you read this. Think of the many things you have always wanted to do but you continually find excuses to avoid them. Sometimes, it's because you've never prioritized it, other times you're just nervous about trying something new. Life becomes boring when we don't take any risks.

I'm curious, what's a dream that you keep putting off? Have you always wanted to learn a new language? What about taking up salsa dancing? Do you want to improve your public speaking? Would you like to start a side business? Volunteer for a charity that is near and dear to your heart? Tell someone you love them?

We hold ourselves back so easily. We allow excuses and the voice of our inner critic to stop us from really living. Stop for a moment and ask, what's the worst that will happen if I fail? Maybe you'll skin your knees or scratch your pride. But I'm sure you will be able to handle it.

Your heart will be beating as you step forward and take your leap. You will feel that proud rush of accomplishment!!! You will feel energized, confident and ready for the next challenge.

I double dog dare you to grab your courage and take a leap. Answer these writing prompts.

What leap will you take today?

____

____

____

____

____

What leap will you take this week?

Come back after you take the leap and capture how you felt. What was the result?

DAY 11
Eliminate Limiting Beliefs

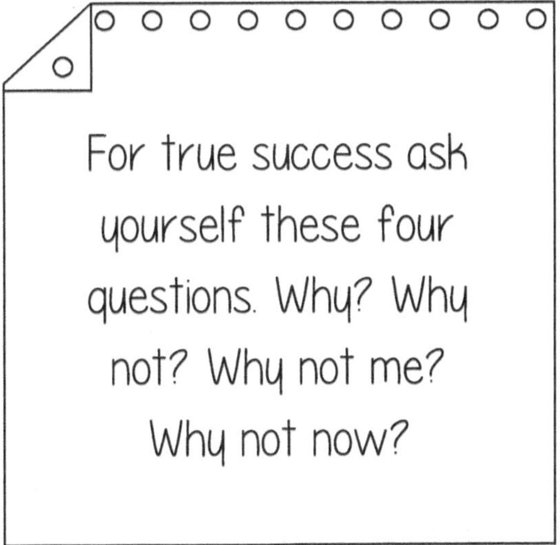

Many people hold themselves back from doing things they would love to do. We can always find an excuse. Here's a common version that I hear all the time with my clients. I call it the "I'm too old / I'm too young" paradox.

How often do you say, I'm too old to do that!!! Do any of these sound familiar?

I'm too old to wear that outfit!

I'm too old to learn how to speak Spanish.

I'm way too old to start my own business.

I'm too old to learn to dance.

The other end of the spectrum is the "I'm too young" excuse.

I'm too young to be promoted.

I'm too young to be taken seriously.

I'm too young to settle down and get married.

I've found that for every "I'm too old", there is an "I'm too young" belief. It's as if we never allow ourselves to live the life we want without this filter. What would happen if you didn't decide based on how society might view our actions?

Where do you say I'm too old or I'm too young? Write them below or in your Soul Journal

____

____

____

____

____

Now ask yourself. How old is the right age to do this? Are you worried someone will laugh at you?

____

____

____

____

____

Whose opinion is it that you're too old or you're too young? Is it your Inner Critic speaking?

____

____

____

____

____

What makes this opinion valid?

____

____

____

____

____

How would you feel if you opted to take action anyway? Would you feel happy / stretched / challenged?

____

____

____

____

____

If you don't act, how much will you regret it?

What have you learned from these questions?

WHAT WOULD HAPPEN IF YOU DIDN'T DECIDE HOW TO LIVE BASED ON HOW SOCIETY MIGHT VIEW YOUR ACTIONS? WHAT WOULD BE POSSIBLE FOR YOU?

DAY 12
Meditation: Mindful Breathing

Mediation is a silent heart
a peaceful mind which
can make life more
lovable, more livable.

Have a stressful meeting coming up? Kids driving you up the wall? Try this mindful breathing meditation that I recorded for you. It's simple, practical and short. You can do it anywhere and in five minutes reset and refresh. Oh and by the way...it makes you feel good.

Practice this meditation at least once per day for seven days. Take time to notice each day in your Soul Journal the effect of meditation. Do you feel more or less relaxed?

YOU CAN LISTEN
TO IT BY GOING TO
THE LINK TO ACCESS
THE FREE RESOURCE.

HTTPS://BIT.LY/2RWPRFY

DAY 13
Turn It Off

We spend too much time connected and online.

When you take a full day away from the TV, your smartphone and social media you will be amazed at how much time you suddenly have available to do other things. Instead of checking Facebook, Instagram or your email every fifteen minutes you can decompress and relax. You will find enough time to read that book you've been meaning to get to. There may also be time for conversation during dinner with your family. It's amazing how much time we devote to our electronics. How much time do you spend flipping channels looking for a decent show to watch or getting lost in your Instagram feed?

Years ago, when my kids were small, I punished my son with no TV for a week. The first day was especially hard because we had to break the habit, talk to each other (gasp) and find something else to do. Surprisingly, it didn't take long to remember how much we enjoyed doing puzzles, playing cards and all the hobbies that were left behind when we were glued to the screen. A few days later and we realized weren't even missing the TV. We decided to do our TV holiday every couple of months because it was rewarding. What was once a punishment turned into a wonderful time for us to reconnect.

WHAT DAY WILL YOU CHOOSE? MAKE YOUR COMMITMENT HERE IN YOUR SOUL JOURNAL

DAY 14
How Do You Spend Your Time?

Wouldn't it be refreshing to spend more time doing the things you <u>want to do</u> and feeling more productive and fulfilled?

Often, we are so busy, but we don't know exactly what we do with all our time. The only way to find out is to do a time audit. It's time to expose those hidden time wasters once and for all. You may find the time to have more fun, enjoy a hobby, or start a side hustle. This exercise takes courage.

Fill in the following chart for a few days. (There's a PDF Printable copy of this chart in your Free Resources Library. To get your copy go here: https://bit.ly/2RWpRfY)

ACTIVITIES	Day 1	Day 2	Day 3	Day 4	Day 5
GROOMING					
MORNING					
NIGHT					
OTHER					
WORK					
COMMUTE					
AT WORK					
PREPARING FOR OR THINKING ABOUT WORK					
GENERAL LIFE					
GROCERY SHOPPING					
COOKING					
CLEANING					
CHORES / LAUNDRY					
RUNNING ERRANDS					

14

ACTIVITIES	Day 1	Day 2	Day 3	Day 4	Day 5
NAGGING AND GRUMBLING					
BANKING/PAYING BILLS / INVESTMENTS					
SLEEP					
PERSONAL TIME LEISURE AND RECREATION					
EXERCISE					
WATCHING TV					
VIDEO GAMES					
FRIENDS					
READING					
SPIRITUAL (INCL MEDITATION, PRAYER, CHURCH)					
HOBBIES/ ACTIVITIES					
PERSONAL EMAIL/ SOCIAL MEDIA					

ACTIVITIES	Day 1	Day 2	Day 3	Day 4	Day 5
PHONE TIME					
QUALITY TIME WITH PARTNER					
FAMILY TIME					
OTHER					
SHOPPING					
SIDE HUSTLE					
VOLUNTEERING					
COURSES/ EDUCATION					
PROCRASTINATING					
PERSONAL APPOINTMENTS (DR, HAIR, MASSAGE, ETC.)					
DRIVING					
TOTAL # HOURS ACCOUNTED FOR (OUT OF 24 HOURS):					

ACTIVITIES	Day 1	Day 2	Day 3	Day 4	Day 5
NUMBER OF TIMES I CHECKED					
PERSONAL EMAIL					
FACEBOOK					
INSTAGRAM					
TWITTER					
PINTEREST					

DAY 15
It's A Play Day

> "We don't stop playing
> because we grow old;
> we grow old because
> we stop playing!"
> – George Bernard Shaw

I bet you have all kinds of responsibilities, and people that rely on you for big and little things. Why don't we take a short break today and do something simple, creative and playful? Spending time in casual play will spark your creative ideas, help you chill out and you will find that you are so much more resilient to manage the tough stuff. Play and fun will loosen you up. Being immersed in play really gets the flow of energy moving in your body and your life

I hosted a seminar for a group of professional women some time ago. We talked about leading with emotional intelligence and avoiding burn out. I had brought some props with me to use for easy stress reduction hints. The Sanity Saving Play Dough was by far the best part of the presentation. When I handed it out, they visibly relaxed and smiled. Each of the women played with the play dough for the rest of the presentation, they rolled it into balls, flattened it like a pancake, made letters out of it and sometimes just squished it through their fingers. It was wonderful to see the joy in their faces when they realized they could take it home at the end of the session.

FRIENDLY WARNING: this is not play dough for your kids this is just for you, but I won't tell if you share it with them too.

SANITY SAVING PLAY DOUGH RECIPE (10 MINUTES)

Ingredients

- » 1 Cup Water.
- » 1 Cup Flour.
- » 2 Tbsp. Cream of Tartar.
- » 2 Tbsp. Vegetable Oil.
- » 2 Tbsp. Table Salt.
- » Food colouring.
- » 10 – 20 drops your favorite essential oil (lavender, bergamot, orange, peppermint, vanilla.)

OPTIONAL: fine craft glitter to add sparkle and shine

Directions

In a heavy saucepan, mix together all ingredients, except for the fragrance.

Using moderate heat, stir continuously. As it thickens, add essential oil. Eventually it will form a ball. Turn the ball out onto a lightly floured board and knead.

Store in an airtight container. It will last for a couple of weeks.

DAY 16
A Reverse To Do List

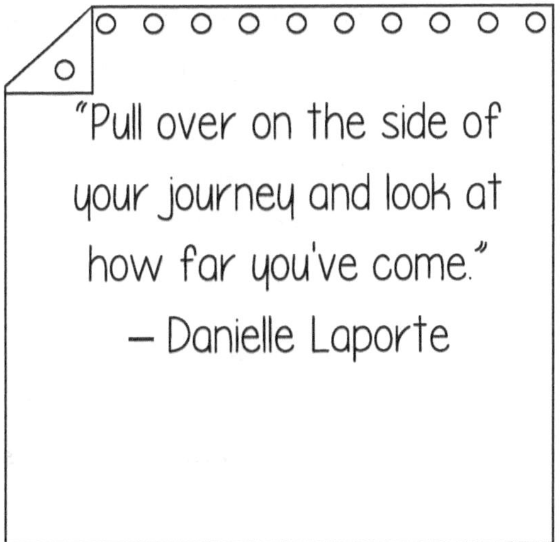

Do you forget to celebrate and savor? Then this is for you.

We spend so much time looking at or thinking about our to do list. Do you feel like you get nothing accomplished and then get bummed out? What if you could turn it around? Today's exercise is a great way to shift your experience.

HERE'S HOW IT WORKS. When you're frustrated dump your regular to do list. Take a new approach. Every time you complete a task, any task, that is satisfying, make a note in a little notebook.

After a few days, you will be amazed when you notice how much better you feel and how much more you've accomplished.

The change in focus from 'not getting enough done' to noticing your progress will improve your perspective.

HERE'S YOUR CHALLENGE. Get yourself a little notebook and keep it close, or use your Soul Journal. Throughout each day, write down the things you complete, especially the ones you are glad you've finished. Your list will be made of up big and small items, maybe you lost five pounds, or you went for a ten-minute walk at lunch. Did you sit down to eat lunch away from your computer? Perhaps you finally completed a big project or ordered the cake for your daughter's birthday party.

If at the end of your day you look at your notebook and find you didn't write down anything, review the day and find at least three things that you completed. A new habit is being established and that takes time! Celebrate your actions and your improvement.

AT THE END OF EACH WEEK: Look at the growing list and choose your top three. Circle or highlight them in your notebook.

Now celebrate. What will you do to reward yourself?

MONTH END: At the end of the month narrow down the top three from each week to your top three for the month.

From time to time, review the entire list. If you wrote down three things each day for a month, the list is now close to one hundred accomplishments long!

CELEBRATE: It's time to celebrate! Let's break the habit of putting ourselves down for all the things we don't do. We frequently bypass the joy of celebration by holding the "don't get enough done" carrot in front of our own noses.

You will find after the first couple of days, you will notice the things you ARE getting done. You will feel better about yourself and appreciate the volume of things you take care of, every single day. You will also be building a new healthy and fun habit of celebrating your achievements. You will feel so much more confident and powerful and present in everything you do.

KEEP A REVERSE TO DO LIST FOR AT LEAST A WEEK BUT PREFERABLY FOR A MONTH TO GET THE MOST BENEFIT.

DAY 17
What Makes Your Heart Sing?

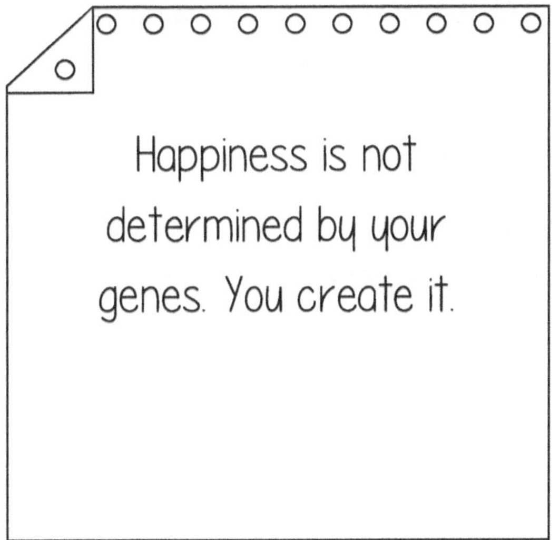

What makes your heart sing? What truly makes you happy? Let's reconnect with delight and cultivate your awareness of joy in some of the simplest things throughout your day. There is joy waiting for you right around every corner. Sometimes, you just forget to look for it

Here's a simple exercise to reconnect with what brings you joy.

Close your eyes and imagine you are truly happy. Conjure up one of your favorite memories or think of the things that always make you happy. Maybe it's a walk on the beach or dinner with friends and family. As you imagine, turn the corners of your mouth up and feel your smile grow. Quietly notice the feeling of joy as it begins to flow through your body. With time and gentle persistence, you will feel absolutely filled to the brim with joy.

Now open your eyes and answer these questions.

Don't filter your thoughts or hold yourself back. Write everything as it comes to you.

THINK BACK TO YOUR CHILDHOOD:

**What brought you the most enjoyment?
Where were you when you were the happiest?
Who were you with?**

THINK BACK TO WHEN YOU WERE A TEENAGER AND YOUNG ADULT:

What brought you joy?
Where were you when you were the happiest?
Who were you with?

THINK BACK TO YOUR RECENT PAST:

What thrills you?
When are you happiest?
Who are you with?
What are you doing?

____

____

____

____

____

____

____

____

____

____

____

____

____

PART 2 THINK OF ALL FIVE SENSES AND RECALL A JOYFUL MEMORY FOR EACH.

√ Smell

√ Sight

√ Taste

√ Touch

√ Sound

NOW ANSWER IN THE TABLE BELOW

For each of your senses. What brings me the most joy? What makes my heart sing?

EXAMPLE: I LOVE THE SMELL OF FLOWERS ON A WARM SPRING EVENING.
EXAMPLE: THE COMFORTING SOUND THE RAIN MAKES ON THE ROOF DURING A STORM.

17

What do you notice as you look at these things that make you happy? Is there a pattern or a theme? Are they easy to do or difficult? Are they expensive or inexpensive?

Finally, what **will** you do today to create more bliss?

18

DAY 18
Create a Digital Vision Board

"The biggest adventure
you can take is to live
the life of your
dreams."
Oprah

It's wonderful to have big dreams and there are lots of different ways to set goals and create your personalized plan to achieve them. One of my favorites is to use a vision board.

Boarding is powerful visualization tool, and a vision board is a great way to capture the essence and the specifics of your dreams and make them a reality. I don't like to go to thrift stores to collect magazines and then cut them up and glue these magazine images to a poster board. I only have a small bit of wall space to put it on and my handwriting is almost illegible.

In a word, my vision board never looks like the beautiful works of art, I see on Pinterest!!!

I'll let you in on a secret. My new FAVORITE way of creating a vision board is digital.

A digital vision board, also known as a dream board, is a collection of images and text that you can take with you wherever you go and it takes less time to create than a physical cork board you stick on the wall. Because they are so easy to make you can make one for each of your goals or one for each of the areas of your entire life!

I spend a lot of time on my computer and phone so having the digital version is much more convenient for me. Since it's digital I can look at my board wherever I am and at any time. This keeps it top of mind so I can always connect with my dreams.

Here are some tips on how you can easily make your own digital vision board and use it to inspire you to reach your dreams and life goals.

STEP 1: Clarify one of your goals. Get super specific about what you really want and why you want to achieve it. Write all the details and pull together a step by step action plan. Ask yourself a few questions that include:

» Who do I need to become to achieve this goal?

» What help will I need?

» What skills will I need to improve?

» How will I keep track of my progress?

» What might get in the way and how can I handle this obstacle?

STEP 2: When deciding what to put on a vision board, use your own photos or search your favorite royalty free websites for images that represent your goals. Photos that you find inspiring and that capture your dreams.

STEP 3: Create your vision board using free online software or an app such as Canva, PicMonkey or PicStitch and make a collage of your inspiring images.

I use Canva most of the time because I can add text in different fonts as overlays to make it even more motivating!

To accomplish this, create a new design, select a collage layout that suits you and then upload the photos you've chosen to the frames. Finally, add some text to further inspire you. The text can be a few simple words, or it can be a written affirmation or goal statement.

For other vision board ideas check out Pinterest. You can spend hours scrolling through gorgeous examples!

STEP 4: Make the graphic the screensaver on your computer desktop and the wallpaper on your smartphone so you see it often. Visions boards work, they influence your subconscious mind! Every time you look at those screens take a moment to remind yourself of your excitement and how good it will be when you reach that goal.

STEP 5: To use this digital vision board to make your dreams a reality, use the photo collage as a reminder to focus intently on your goals and connect with your vision.

To do this, look at your complete vision board first thing in the morning, throughout the day and last thing at night. Imagine, in detail, what your life will be like when you have achieved your goals.

To make your dreams as tangible and realistic as possible, ask yourself:

» How will I feel?

» Who will I be with?

» What temperature will it be?

» What will I be wearing?

» Is there a flavour, colour or scent?

And most importantly remember that to achieve your goals you start with a commitment, create an action plan (break it down into small achievable steps), be ready and open to opportunities that show up.

GOALS WILL NEVER
COME TRUE IF ALL YOU
DO IS DREAM ABOUT
THEM. YOU'VE GOT TO
VISUALIZE IT, STAY
FOCUSED, DO THE
WORK AND TAKE
INSPIRED ACTION TO
MAKE THEM A REALITY.

DAY 19
Eliminate Hidden Time Wasters

Have you heard the story of the teacher who stands at the front of the class and does a demonstration?

She has a big glass pitcher, and in it she puts a bunch of big rocks. She asks the class. "Is this pitcher full?"

Then she adds a bunch of sand. The grains fill in between the rocks and again she asks. "Now, is this pitcher full?"

Once more she takes a glass of water and pours it into the pitcher. The water fills in all the nooks and crannies. "Now the pitcher is full?"

On Day 14 you started your time audit. If you've never done this before, I'm sure you're surprised where you spend your most precious resource. Your time. If you fell behind in doing your time audit, don't worry, use this day as a gentle reminder to keep with it. You are making amazing progress!

In this story, the big rocks are your top priorities, the sand are those things that are important and needed. The water represents the busy things you do, neither very important and frequently not even urgent.

Where is your time and energy spent? On the big rocks, the sand or the water?

Do you have goals and intentions that are important, and find you give them little time and effort? These goals and dreams should be your big rocks and they need to be placed first to they get your focus and attention.

Unearthing Your Big Rocks

» Have you always wanted to start your own small business?

» Do you wish you could travel more?

» Would you love to write a book?

» Are you keen to run a 10k race or a marathon?

» Do you want to start a family?

» Do you dream of going back to school and finishing your degree?

List your big rocks in your Soul Journal.

Where do you currently spend most of your time? (use your time audit from Day 14 to help you fill this in):

____

____

____

____

What is the single biggest time waster you have?

____

____

____

____

Is there a gap between your biggest priorities and how you spend your time?

____

____

____

____

What must change to free up more time to pursue your priorities?

____

____

____

____

____

SOME EXAMPLES: Book a house cleaner. Grocery shop only once per week. Limit the time you spend watching TV or scrolling through social media. Hire a babysitter once a week so you and your partner can have some time together. If money is tight consider swapping with a friend or family member.

What will you gain by freeing up more time?

____

____

____

____

____

DAY 20
Get Honest and Unstuck

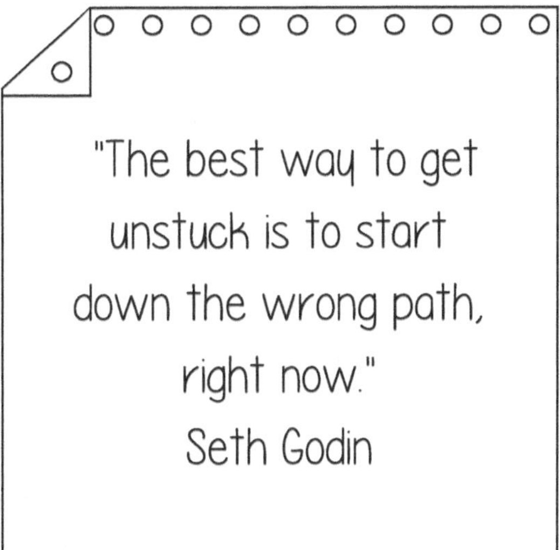

Ok, you're stuck. Lots of times when we're stuck it's because we've forgotten we are in control of our attitude, behaviour and ultimately our lives. I know it's hard to hear, but sometimes we even ignore the truth about how we got into this situation.

Here are five steps to help you move forward and change your circumstances.

STEP 1: The first step is acceptance! No longer resisting, struggling or wishing it was different. Accepting the situation for what it is.

Practice acceptance. Surrender and breathe. Right now, set a time for five minutes to breathe. Notice this is where you are right now, release the fight and relax. Once you feel centered and calm you're ready to tackle the next step.

STEP 2: Get curious. Take a courageous inventory of your choices and your current situation. Where did you ignore the truth and forge ahead anyway?

Did you choose the wrong person to get involved with? Your gut was whispering to you, but you decided to go ahead and get involved anyway. Now you're not sure how to leave the relationship.

Did you accept that new job, even though you had some misgivings at the time? Now you feel stuck and want your old job back.

I bet you probably knew you shouldn't have bought the most expensive furniture on a payment plan? But you wanted your new place to be impressive, and now you're stuck with the bill for five years.

STEP 3: Now, that you've faced the truth, give yourself a pat on the back. It takes courage to look honestly at your circumstances. I am proud of you and you should be proud of yourself too!

STEP 4: The next step, take some quiet time and answer these questions.

What's your biggest worry if you made a change?

____

____

____

What are you avoiding by staying stuck?

How are you cheating yourself by not being decisive?

What dreams are you putting on hold by avoiding action?

What do you have to release to move forward towards the life you were born to live?

These are not easy questions. But as Your Personal Life Coach I trust that you know the answers. You are courageous and this clarity you are developing will lead you to your best fulfilled and empowered life.

STEP 5: Listen to your Inner Mentor, it is quietly whispering the truth. Spirit wants nothing more than for you to have a life filled with satisfaction, dreams, joy and abundance.

DAY 21
One Hundred Things
That Make You Proud

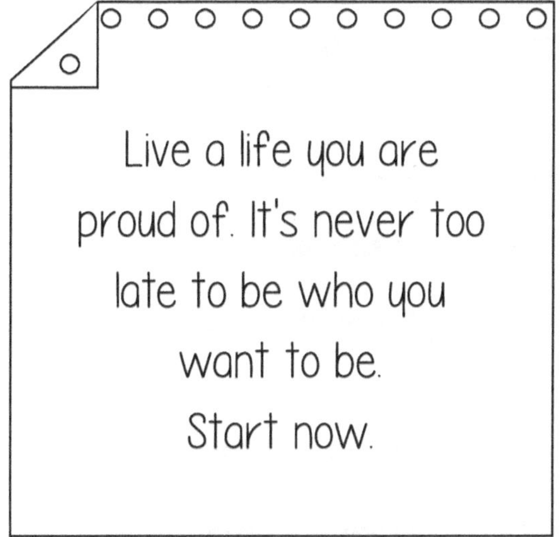

It's time for a challenge. A one hundred challenge!

It is time to reconnect with the wonder of you! You might get down on yourself and feel like you have nothing to contribute and maybe feel like you've never accomplished much. People generally have a short memory when it comes to the things we appreciate about ourselves. If you don't feel good about yourself how can you have the confidence to tackle a challenge or to set a goal and reach it?

Here's what to do. Grab your Soul Journal and fill in one hundred things that make you feel proud about yourself.

They can be big or small it doesn't matter. You may find you have trouble remembering all the things you've achieved, so give it time.

Carry your trusty Soul Journal around with you and add to it every time you remember something. Once you get moving, you will find it gets easier.

Here's some ideas to get your started:

√ **Graduated from high school.**

√ **Told Jim I would NOT organize the Summer BBQ for work this year.**

√ **Traveled to South East Asia for three months.**

√ **Did a 30-day meditation challenge.**

√ **Went to therapy for my depression.**

√ **Got rid of my credit card debt.**

√ **Saved $1000.**

√ **Recognized at work for doing a great job on the Smith account.**

√ **Quit smoking.**

√ **Accepted to medical school.**

√ **Passed my French class.**

√ **Went to my first yoga class.**

√ **Planted a garden and grew vegetables for the first time.**

√ **Learned how to bake bread from scratch.**

√ **Learned how to knit.**

√ **Lost 5lbs.**

√ **Lost 100 lbs.**

√ **Ran a 10k.**

√ **Ran my first half marathon.**

√ **Sat with my sister in the hospital as she recovered from surgery (and I hate hospitals).**

√ **Became a vegetarian.**

√ **Asked for a raise.**

√ **Got a promotion.**

√ **Stood up for myself against a bully.**

√ **Told my boyfriend "I love you" for the first time.**

√ **Went bungee jumping.**

√ **Sponsored a child.**

GET STARTED NOW. GRAB YOUR SOUL JOURNAL AND WRITE:

DAY 22
Shift Beyond Stuck

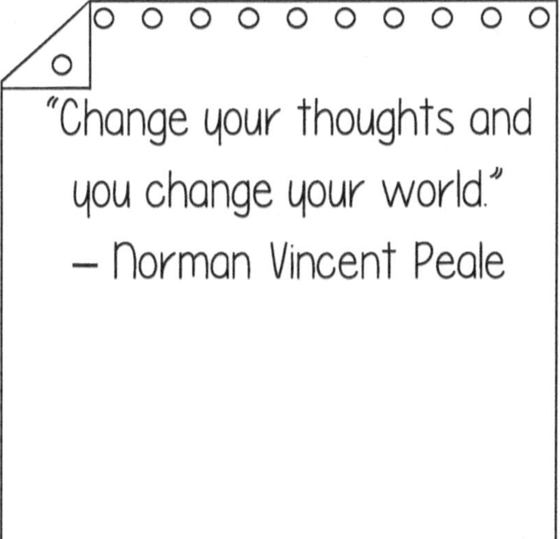

It's amazing how habits are developed. Our brain likes to run on automatic wherever possible. This saves energy and subconsciously means we have to think less. Sometimes this is good. Remember when you learned to drive? It took a lot of concentration to check your mirrors, turn on the windshield wipers and brake for a red light all at the same time. With practice now, you can manage all those little details easily and automatically. Sometimes habits are useful and healthy. But always living on automatic can lead you to getting stuck in a rut.

I realized many years ago, when I used to commute downtown for my corporate job that I would always drive in the curb lane until I reached a certain intersection, then I would change to the middle lane and eventually make my way into the centre lane. Finally I would make *exactly* the same left turn every day.

I saw the same sights every single day. No wonder I felt stuck, and bored. There was nothing fresh in my life. I was living like a robot.

What about you? Do you take the same route to work every day? Do you eat at the same restaurants and visit the same places? Do you always go to the same exercise class and park in the same area when you go shopping?

For the next week, try something out of the ordinary. Eat lunch in a new spot. Rearrange your furniture. Add something new to your desk. Wear more makeup or do your hair differently. Change the way you move through life. Who knows what will happen? You might meet someone new, or maybe get a new perspective. These small easy shifts can get you unstuck quickly and easily.

Capture the results of these small changes in your Soul Journal.

The changes I made:

____

____

____

____

____

____

How do you feel?

115

What's different? What's the same?

What new things are you seeing?

What opportunities are available to you now?

DAY 23
Clear The Clutter

We are a consumer society. We are surrounded by stuff, and it is overwhelming. Clutter is often the biggest contributor to confusion. Clutter can be things we own, too many apps on our smart phone, too many email newsletter subscriptions, unorganized computer files and photos. All these things contribute to our overload.

Today is a great day to begin clearing the clutter! Let go of things you don't need or no longer want. It is liberating. I remember once I was doing some house sitting for a family before Netflix was popular. It was common to have a collection of DVDs. I was looking through their movie collection and realized there were more than twenty movies unopened. They even had doubles and triples of the same movies. Frankly, when I opened that cupboard everything was a mess and it was confusing.

Having spent time in that environment motivated me to examine my own home.

Once I got home I found I had new clothes, that still had the tags attached, bought months prior. There were disorganized piles of magazines and books that needed clearing too. Then it was time for the kitchen, how many casserole dishes and partially opened packages of food and spices did we really need? This turned into a whirlwind of purging and we've never looked back. We're not minimalists, but now we are careful about what we have.

Start small. Try a 15-minute clutter challenge!

Today your challenge is to choose *one* area of your life and clear the clutter. It could be the bathroom cupboards or your computer files, it doesn't matter what it is. Start by choosing the easiest area and go for it!!! When you're complete, stand back and look at it. Don't you feel refreshed, empowered and clear?

24

DAY 24
Let Go Of The Past

Our past can keep us prisoner. Living in the past reinforces limiting beliefs.

Do you spend much of your time reminiscing about events in the past? Are all your good times in the past? These old beliefs can keep you stuck. Don't let what's happened in the past hold you back any longer.

Whatever you're holding on to can stand in your way of living your best life. Learning how to let go will help you to release these blocks. What do you need to let go of? Who do you need to forgive? Sometimes the person most in need of forgiveness is **you**.

Letting go doesn't mean you pretend everything didn't happen, it's a lightening of your load, a releasing of the ties that bind you to past events that you no longer have control over.

You don't need to know how to let go, **you only need to be willing to let go and be willing to forgive.** You know you can't change the past, but you can forgive and learn from it.

Create a list in your Soul Journal of the things you need to release:

____

____

____

____

____

Ask yourself who will benefit from releasing the hold these past events have on you?

____

____

____

____

Imagine you have released everything on this list. What would life be like for you?

____

____

____

____

Now which of these things are you willing to release?

» I am now willing to forgive and release...

____

____

____

____

What possibilities or opportunities are available to you now?

____

____

____

____

25

DAY 25
Take A Mindful Walk Outside

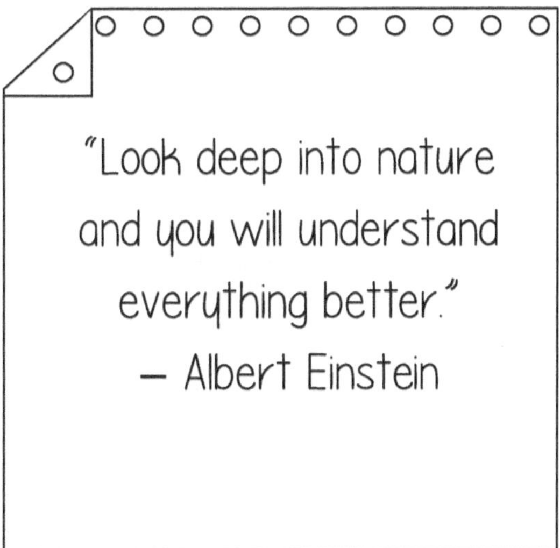

Today, for fifteen minutes, put on your jacket and go for a walk outside in nature. Find a park, a trail or a beach and leisurely stroll for fifteen minutes. Be fully present and leave your phone at home.

Meander slowly, this isn't about covering ground or getting in your step count for the day. Stroll and notice all the different things that you can take in with your five senses. Observe as many positive things as possible.

Here are some prompts to use when you stroll:

» What scents do you notice?

» What do you see?

» What colour is the sky?

» Notice the fine detail of the leaves on the trees and underfoot.

» Look at the myriad of colours. Green, blue, brown, white and grey.

» Is the sunlight dancing on the water?

» What do the shadows look like?

» What is it to feel the rain or sun shining on your face?

Pause for a moment as you hear or see each impression and make sure it registers with your conscious awareness. Really savour it. Try to identify what it is about that thing that makes it pleasurable to you.

26

DAY 26
Learn How To Apologize

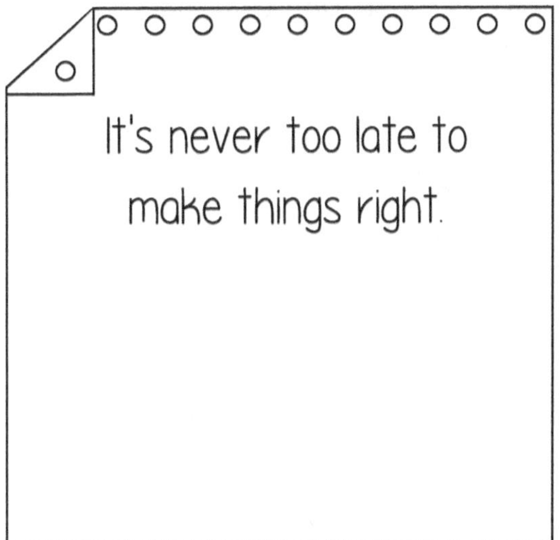

Oh no!!! You've made a mistake, either you've said something or done something, and you've wronged someone. Today is a good day to learn how to take personal responsibility and apologize to make amends.

There are four parts to an effective apology.

STEP 1: ACKNOWLEDGE THE OFFENSE AND MAKE IT SPECIFIC. Taking personal responsibility makes a good apology effective. Apologies are more likely to be well-received if you show that you recognize who was responsible, who was harmed, and the nature of the offense.

When you say "I said something hurtful" instead of "hurtful things were said" it makes a deeper emotional connection with the person who has been wronged. Be straightforward not vague. "I'm sorry for that mean joke I made yesterday "carries more impact than "I'm sorry you feel hurt". This second sentence puts the responsibility on the victim for being hurt.

STEP 2: SOMETIMES AN EXPLANATION CAN HELP. But be careful sometimes an explanation sounds like you're making excuses. An explanation can be helpful if you are wanting to explain that it wasn't intentional. For example, "it wasn't intentional, and it will not happen again".

STEP 3: EXPRESS REMORSE. When you hurt someone, it's natural to feel shame, humiliation, or remorse. Expressing these feelings shows that you recognize and regret the suffering you caused. Acknowledge your disappointment in yourself and your commitment to improve.

STEP 4: MAKE AMENDS. A good apology should include efforts to repair the damage done. When considering how to best make amends, be sure to ask the offended person what would mean the most to them, rather than simply doing something to relieve your own feelings of guilt.

We all need to learn how to apologize when we are wrong, or we've done something to hurt someone. Once you know you're in the wrong, use these four steps to craft the best apology for the situation.

DAY 27
Journal Your Way To Inner Peace

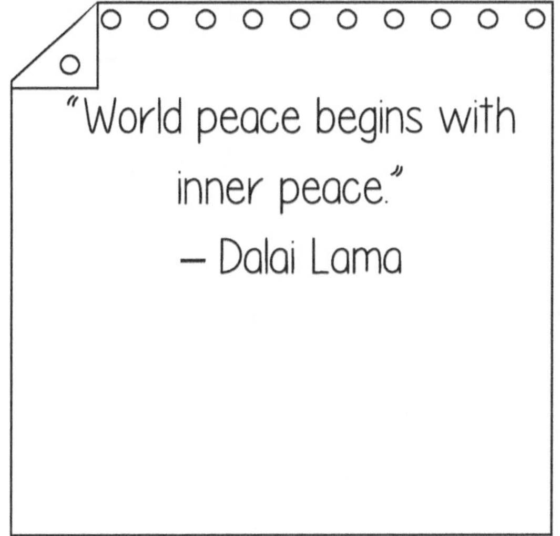

When you are angry, sad or frustrated it's easy to spend hours or even days reliving the problem. You can allow the problem to consume you it spins endlessly in your imagination. Continual worry ruins your life and leads to sleepless nights or stressful days. How can you move past this and reclaim your equilibrium? One of my favorite ways is to clear my emotions through a written journal.

Start by finding a quiet place where you won't be disturbed. If you've got a busy home, you can complete this task sitting in a park or in your car.

For this type of journaling I don't use my Soul Journal. Instead, I use blank or lined paper loose paper.

1. Write the problem at the top of a page.

2. Now, set a timer for fifteen minutes. Write for the full fifteen minutes. Even when you run out of things to say, continue to write. Rehash thoughts, you've already written. If you run out of things to say, you can write over and over "I'm so angry", "I'm so frustrated" "this is stupid", even "AAARGH". Whatever comes to mind is allowed. During this time, give yourself permission to be totally immersed in that emotion. Write hard, write fast, fully vent. If you swear and cry, that's ok! Stick with it. Don't worry about spelling errors or grammar mistakes. The purpose is to vent, get it out of your mind and onto that paper

3. If the timer sounds and you have more to say (which is rare, fifteen minutes of writing is a LOT), then set the timer for an additional ten minutes and keep writing to the end of that time slot.

4. The final step, destroy what you've written. Treat it as the closing steps of a ritual. Put the papers through the shredder, burn them in the fireplace. Whatever is appropriate for you, this final step allows you to release the emotions and the hold they have over you.

DAY 28
The Most Powerful Word. NO!

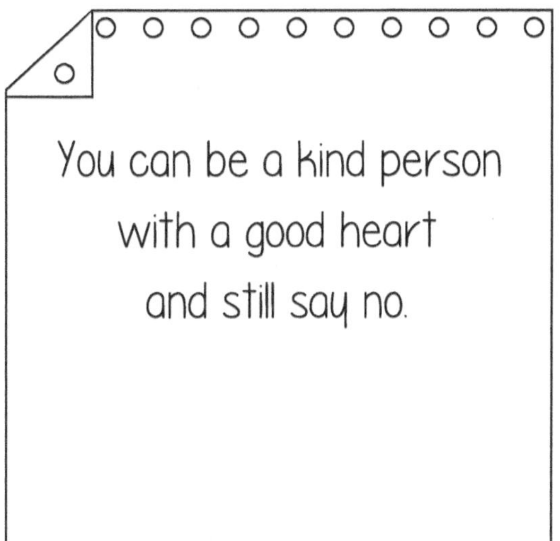

Do you feel overloaded? Is the weight of the world on your shoulders? Have you got more to do than you have hours in a day? My guess, you are incredibly adept at juggling a million balls. But now that you're juggling a million and one it may be too much. Now with that one extra ball you are slipping. You've dropped first one ball, then another. Oops you forgot your sister in law's birthday. Then you forgot to pay the property taxes on time. Crap, crap crap!!! It's no fun, and frankly, it can be exhausting trying to keep all those balls in the air.

Many high achievers feel the need to do it all themselves. They welcome all the responsibilities, tasks, projects. You know what

I mean, you're part of the "sandwich generation" caring for both your elders, children and sometimes grandchildren too. Then there is the cleaning, cooking and grocery shopping. More than likely you host Thanksgiving <u>and</u> Christmas dinner every year too. You accomplish all of these things and at the same time you are creating your business plan, refining the financial forecast for this quarter and providing input on a proposal for a new contract. Then you pick up your sick kid from school and talk to your disappointed teenager who didn't get picked for the soccer team and finally respond to emails until 11pm.

Maybe it's time to learn a new skill. How to say 'no'.

Think of a two-year-old. That face, the defiant stance, the powerful energy when they say it. "NO!!!" It's simple, not laced with excuses and niceties. They are fully standing in their power. You can recapture some of your power today and stake a claim for your two-year-old self. I'm curious, what is it you <u>really</u> don't want to do anymore?

Take out a pen and paper and write them here. Write with abandon. This is for your eyes only!

____

____

____

____

____

Now choose a couple from the list that you really dread. Here's the key, the next time someone asks you to take their turn driving the car pool, look after their place while they're away on vacation, or help on a new, and very boring, strategic initiative. Take the leap and practice saying "No".

Have some fun and get creative, list all the ways you can decline. You can be gentle, nice, nasty, firm or straightforward. Here are some ideas to start you off:

» No
» NO!!!
» Hell no!
» Forget it.
» Not me.
» Are you kidding me?
» Absolutely not!
» Not right now.
» Let me sleep on it and get back to you.
» No thanks.
» Not at this time.
» It's not right for me.
» I'll pass.
» I'm going to have to say no because...
» Thanks for thinking of me, but I'm going to say no.

The next time someone asks you to do something that you either don't have time for or just don't want to do. I encourage you to practice your new skill and decline.

IT TAKES TIME AND PRACTICE TO MAKE NEW HABITS. SO, PRACTICE LOTS... PRACTICE IN THE MIRROR, PRACTICE IN YOUR CAR, PRACTICE IN PERSON. JUST PRACTICE!

DAY 29
You Deserve A Play Day

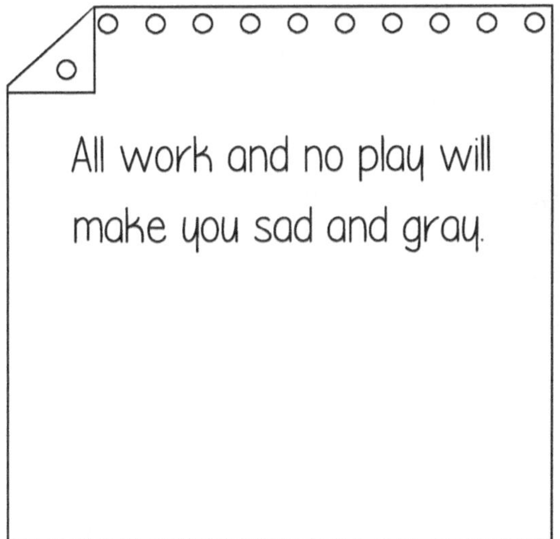

It's time for a second play day. How much did you enjoy the play dough? Did everyone get in on the act? Today, let's do some simple crafting.

Here are four fun ideas to try that also support your self care. They are all quick to do and many of these ingredients you've probably got around your home.

Don't hold back, dive in. See how you feel once you're done. We get so stuck in having to be artistically talented we don't let ourselves relax, let go and enjoy. Remember, being immersed in play really gets the flow of energy moving in your body and your life.

CALMING GLITTER JAR

It's like a meditation snow globe. This one you can keep in your desk drawer for those dreaded conference calls

It's simple to make, all you need is:

» A screw top jar. I use a mason jar.

» 1-2 tablespoons of glitter glue.

» 3-4 teaspoons of glitter.

» Hot (not boiling) water.

» A drop of food colouring.

Fill the jar with hot water. Leave some space at the top. Add the glitter glue and stir it well so it melts and is completely mixed in. Add the glitter and the food colouring. Screw the lid on tight. Make sure it's well sealed.

SUGAR SCRUB (HONEY AND LEMON)

Perfect for bath or shower time and you will smell divine!

Ingredients

» 1 cup sugar.

» 1/4 cup olive oil.

» 2 Tablespoons raw honey.

» 2 tsp dried rosemary.

» 15 drops lemon essential oil.

» 15 drops lavender essential.

Directions

Mix sugar, dried rosemary, olive oil, and raw honey together. Add essential oils and stir to combine. Store in a glass jar.

SUGAR SCRUB (OATMEAL AND HONEY)

Ingredients

» 1 cup sugar.

» 1/3 cup coconut oil.

» ½ cup oats.

» ¼ cup honey.

» 15 drops orange essential oil.

Directions

Mix all ingredients and stir to combine. Store in a glass jar.

SOOTHING SCENTED COCONUT BATH MELTS

Ingredients

» 1 cup coconut oil.

» 15 drops essential oil.

» Ice cube tray.

Directions

In a double boiler, melt the coconut oil on low heat until melted.

Add essential oil. Mix all ingredients and stir to combine. Pour into ice cube tray

Place in freezer for approximately 20 – 30 minutes until firm

Pop them out of the ice cube tray. Store in a cool air tight container

Add one or two of these nourishing bath melts to a hot bath. Your skin will thank you!

30

DAY 30
Write A Compassionate Letter To Yourself

"When we give ourselves compassion, we are opening our hearts in a way that can transform our lives."
— Kristen Neff

You have made mistakes. Is there something about yourself that you really don't like? Are there times when you feel you are not good enough or are ashamed?

Forgive yourself. Here's how.

This is an exercise for your Soul Journal. Take up your pen and begin writing.

First, identify something about yourself that makes you feel ashamed, insecure, or not good enough. It could be something related to your appearance, personality, behavior, abilities, relationships, or any part of your life.

Once you identify something, write it down and describe how it makes you feel. Sad? Embarrassed? Angry? Be as honest as possible. Remember you are the only one who will see what you've written.

The next step take a few minutes and read what you've written as *if you had written it about your best friend or your child*. Let the impact sink in. Would you ever speak this way to your dearest friend?

Now, write a new letter to yourself expressing compassion, understanding, and acceptance for that same scenario or characteristic that you dislike.

Imagine you are writing from the perspective of someone who loves and accepts you exactly as you are right now. Remind yourself that everyone has flaws. Imagine the countless other people who might be struggling with the same situation.

What would this compassionate observer say?

Kindly ask yourself whether there are ways you could improve? What constructive steps could you take to feel happier and less judgemental?

Write these specific steps you will take.

Once you're done, re-read the second compassionate observer letter. This time read it as if you are reading about someone else. Be as kind, supportive and forgiving as you would be to a friend.

THE NEXT TIME YOU ARE
FEELING BAD ABOUT THIS SAME
SITUATION OR ASPECT OF
YOURSELF, RE-READ THE LETTER
FROM THAT COMPASSIONATE
OBSERVER PERSPECTIVE AND
NOTICE WHERE YOU FEEL
A LITTLE KINDER, MORE
FORGIVING TOWARDS
YOURSELF.

DAY 31
Take Yourself On A Date

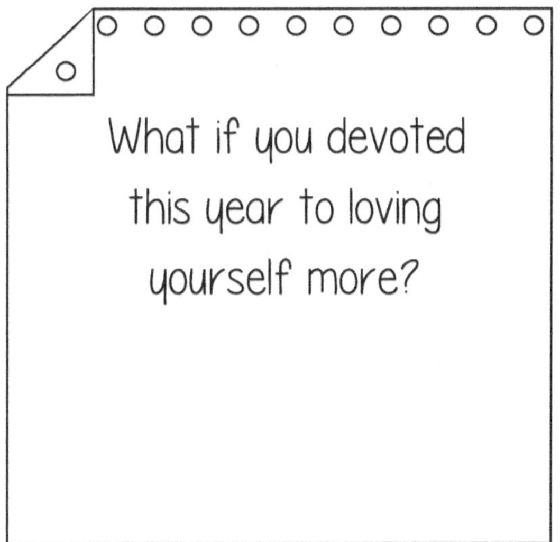

Spend an afternoon or an evening doing exactly what you want to do, whatever it is that totally makes you happy. Do it by yourself, or a good friend, so you don't have to compromise.

Plan it in detail, sketch it out. Circle a date in the not to distant future. Write out all the details in your Soul Journal.

Here are some prompts to get you started

» How would the day start?
» What will you wear?
» Will you go out for breakfast, coffee, lunch?

» What about going to live theatre or a movie?
» Where will you go? Is there a gorgeous farmers market or boutique store you've been itching to go to? Or do you want to pack a picnic lunch and spend the day at the beach reading a juicy novel?
» How will you pamper yourself?

Imagine the perfect day in detail and write everything down. Nothing is too crazy or too wild to plan in your day. Once you've run out of ideas, come back to it from time to time and add more ideas.

Once you got your perfect day planned. Which of these things will you choose to do this time? Make a commitment to yourself and enjoy your day.

CAPTURE YOUR DAY WITH LOTS OF PHOTOS, COPIES OF TICKET STUBS, ANY MEMENTO THAT YOU ENJOY. RELIVE THE DAY FROM TIME TO TIME AND REMEMBER THE FUN YOU HAD.

CONCLUSION

CONGRATULATIONS, YOU'VE MADE IT TO THE END OF THE 31 DAYS AND 31 WAYS. THANK YOU FOR JOINING ME IN THIS JOURNEY.

Now that the program is complete, return to page 5, "Start Here" and repeat The Wheel of Life exercise. I'm curious to know what's changed? Where has your life become more satisfying? Where is it the same?

I can't wait to hear about your experience. How has the Say YES to Your Best Life: 31-Days to Clarity, Confidence and Contentment journey been for you? Were you able to complete all the exercises? If not, why not?

Which of the days gave you the biggest breakthrough or "aha" moment? What did you learn from it? What have you taken away?

P.S. IF YOU HAVEN'T ALREADY, DOWNLOAD THE FREE RESOURCES THAT I CREATED SO YOU CAN GET THE MOST OUT OF THIS BOOK BY GOING TO **HTTPS://BIT.LY/2RWPRFY.**

ABOUT THE AUTHOR

Human BEING, wife, mother, family member, friend, nature lover, dancer, dreamer, barefoot leader, authentic introvert, sacred rebel, joy seeker.

She is trained as an engineer and has held every level of job from entry level, through to senior corporate director for one of the largest real estate management companies worldwide. Candy leverages this real-world experience with her coaching clients.

She holds coaching credentials from the International Coaching Federation and was trained at the Harvard of coach training, The Coaches Training Institute. Her clients are women and men from all walks of life, with this common thread: they want a better life and they know the fastest way to get it is through coaching.

As Your Personal Life Coach, Candy works with brilliant people to create a breakthrough in skills and mindset, significantly improving their satisfaction, performance and results. At the heart of her work is a passion for empowering people to reach their full potential. She support people to understand who they are at their best, and get clear on blind spots that impede their success so they can thrive.

She has written this book to impact more people. So many people want to be happy and successful and Candy knows that working one on one with a coach can be expensive. Years ago, she decided her mission was to help as many people as she can. Her goal is to encourage you to live the life you were born to live. This is how

Candy became Your Personal Life Coach. **It's a way for you to coach virtually with her right now, even if it's 4 am.**

Candy's goal is to motivate and empower you to play bigger in your lives.

Since she can't talk to most of you face to face, Candy encourages you to follow her on all social media channels and on her website. It's where she personally encourages and speaks to people every day.